Beside You at the Stoplight

Beside
You

at the Stoplight

Marjorie Saiser

The Backwaters Press

Also by Marjorie Saiser

Rooms, Pudding House Publications, 2010
Moving On, Lone Willow Press, 2002
Lost in Seward County, The Backwaters Press, 2001
Bones of a Very Fine Hand, The Backwaters Press, 1999

Photo of the poet courtesy of the poet.
Cover art "Browns & Blacks" by Marjorie Saiser, © 2010.
Photo of cover art by Karen Shoemaker.
Cover design by Bristol Creative, www.bristolcreative.com.
Book design by The Backwaters Press.
All poems © 2010 Marjorie Saiser unless otherwise noted.

First Printing: October 2010

2009 Winner of the Little Blue Stem Award in Poetry

Beside You at the Stoplight is printed as a cooperative effort between the Nebraska Arts Council and The Backwaters Press, in order to honor the winners of the Nebraska Arts Council's Distinguished Artist Awards. Marjorie Saiser won the Distinguished Artist Award for 2009, which included a cash award of $5,000 and the publication of this book.

Published by: The Backwaters Press
3502 N 52nd Street
Omaha, NE 68104-3506
Greg Kosmicki & Rich Wyatt, Editors

http://www.thebackwaterspress.org
thebackwaterspress@gmail.com

ISBN: 978-1-935218-17-3

Acknowledgments

Crab Orchard Review: "Template"

Cream City Review: "Even the Alphabet"

Laurel Review: "You Wonder Why We Can't Get Along"

Prairie Schooner: "From Her White Knuckles," "On the Road," "Paradise on the Niobrara," "My Father Argued with My Mother," "Walking the Baby," "For My Body" reprinted from *Prairie Schooner* volume 81 issue 2 (Summer 2007) by permission of the University of Nebraska Press. Copyright 2007 by the University of Nebraska Press.
"I Want to Be a Man" reprinted from *Prairie Schooner* volume 75 issue 3 (Fall 2001) by permission of the University of Nebraska Press. Copyright 2001 by the University of Nebraska Press.
"Mammogram" reprinted from *Prairie Schooner* volume 73 issue 2 (Summer 1999) by permission of the University of Nebraska Press. Copyright 1999 by the University of Nebraska Press.
"To the Statue of the Scribe in the Museum" reprinted from *Prairie Schooner* volume 79 issue 4 (Winter 2005) by permission of the University of Nebraska Press. Copyright 2005 by the University of Nebraska Press.

qarrtsiluni: " Here's to My Legs"

Beside You at the Stoplight

I.

II.

III.

for Don, again

I

You and I, the Cranes, the River

The cranes were silhouettes that night, thousands
lowering in long strings to land in the river.
We stood at peepholes in a shed on the bank,
silent, watching. And I began to wish
someone could see us, witness us,
you and I,
durable in our heavy coats and scarves,
looking out into the dark.
We were not jaded then.
Nothing remarkable happened for an hour,
no talking; we didn't want to spook the cranes
standing on their sandbars, trilling their
all-night song. Then you pointed
toward a peephole in the western wall,
turned my shoulders, mouthed a word,
one word. Vapor rose from your mouth. *Moon*, you said.
And we looked at it together, a thin white curved tusk,
a filament, a lost string, a moon on its back.
At a small window we looked at the moon together.

Weekends, Sleeping In

No jump-starting the day,
no bare feet slapping the floor
to bath and breakfast.

Dozing instead
in the nest
like, I suppose,
a pair of gophers

underground
in fuzz and wood shavings.
One jostles the other
in closed-eye luxury.

We are at last
perhaps
what we are:

uncombed,
unclothed,
mortal.

Pulse
and breath
and dream.

The Spark That Flows Between Us

Our hands swinging as we walk side by side
our knuckles sometimes barely touching
we walk our two miles
our two miles of putting one foot in front of the other
your long legs' long reach
my short shanks

you carry my bottle of water
you carry more than that

you carry
and I carry
some mornings into the second mile
something electric

hanging around

you, me

a few electrons brushed from the bottom of the shoe
give their charge to the larger body

so huge a leap

a small moon leaves its orbit

becomes part of something new

the gift of friction
the big bang all over again

the spark that flows between us.

Two Games and Shoes, Six Bucks

Don't have the arm I used to
(but who does?)

and we are bowling,
my heartthrob and I.

Here am I at one end of a hardwood trail,
and at the other, the fat pins sit

like the sitting ducks they are.
I'm concentrating

not on the arm or the aim
I used to have

but on the head pin and its next-door neighbor.
I'm concentrating on how my hero

racks up those big X's in a row
(the screen overhead tells all the world)

concentrating on how good he looks from behind
concentrating on the sweet smack of the pins—

the exquisite noise
when all ten fly up in a flock

and mix and suspend.
It's my turn, arm or no arm,

and my baby-blue ball
rolls over and over

like the years, the inescapable years,
leaving me watching,

hoping,
dancing on one foot,

hand in the air—
hang in there I tell myself—

use all—and a little bit more—
of what you've got left.

Sometimes I Stray Deliberately

Sometimes I stray deliberately,
leave the sidewalk

to feel the earth give
ever so little because I am here.

Cardinals sing
to say they are passing through,

have found a mate.
Tonight at our table you and I

will pick over our meal
across from one another

like birds on the ground.

Like birds on the ground
we won't say much, as if to say:

This is good, isn't it,
this morsel, this huge life?

Pulling up Beside You at the Stoplight

We are going to the same place
but we take two cars.
Sunday morning and there's not much traffic
so I pull up beside you at the stoplight. There you are
in your car,
beside my car,
your profile in the window,
the brown of your hair against your neck. You turn
and blow me a kiss. I watch it float on by.
I ask for another.

I remember how you come into the dark bedroom
on weekday mornings,
the sound of your work boots across the carpet,
the scent of your face when you find me in the covers,
kiss my eyebrow and the corner of my mouth,
tell me the weather report
and the precise time of day.

So I roll down my window, whistle in my throat,
pull my glasses crooked on my face,
do my best baboon snorting,
pound the horn as if it were bread dough.
There is only the woman in the white Buick
but you are embarrassed, glad to see the green.
I'm stepping on the gas, catching up,

wondering what I can do at 56th and Calvert.

Even the Alphabet

Consider *s*
who stands beside another, close as possible,

c who will not abandon *k* at the end,
no matter how thick the attack,

q who breaks the trail for *u*, who without *u*
can hardly manage what is required—

and consider how letters live in the body,
play in it, against the back of the teeth,

in the wet active tongue,
and make the lips to part, to close.

Consider how necessary silence is,
coupled with constancy,

how silence can make a syllable benign,
so that it does not shout to show valor,

but softly stands in place
and changes everything,

as does *k* who, though it can speak,
kneels before *n* and says nothing, nothing.

You Wonder Why We Don't Get Along

I'm bromegrass, bluestem,
lespedeza like a fur ball in the hand.
Nine-Mile Prairie is my hang-out. I live there,
weekends, with the ticks and the jaybirds,
with the swallow's slow arc
from cedar to cedar.

I'm the Platte, crossing and
re-crossing its own channels.
I'm a prairie liar; I learned to walk
on switchgrass, on cactus,
toddling after
a big man in boots checking on his cattle.
Barefoot—silly baby—I couldn't keep up,

and then his Herefords wheeled and charged.
I'm used to the blank stare.
A snort in the nostrils
my lullaby. I'm running still,

unshod feet
over unplowed ground.
No screams from my mouth: open,
soft as the evening primrose.
Silent, chased by my herd.

Plan

Let your shawl
cover you,
as mine does me.

Let your feathered beaded shawl
swirl about you when you walk,
as mine swirls about me.

Under the shawls, armor
lies heavy on our shoulders,
cold against the skin.

Mine has its chinks and holes,
as yours does,
to let small arrows in.

The Colors of the Trees in Pennsylvania

The leaves were all manner of red,
red against and among
the black branches.

Stunning, I imagine,
but we drove in the dark
toward our destination.

I loved you, the sun came up, the sun
went down, I did not say love properly.

The red of the maple at the roadside,
red which is red quadrupled,
red raised to the tenth power of red,

red present all along, the biologist tells us,
red underneath the green,
red all the time it was green.

Green was its darkness.

When I Dance, You Think to Make Me Sad

I whirl, stepping around the empty room,
my feet weighing less than sparrows,

my soles light against the wood,
body so willing to follow.

Shall I go as if stepping out of winding sheets?
Shall I leave the polished boards gleaming in the dusk?

I am to Dance as yellow is
to a field of mustard flowers.

Don't talk to me, I, over my shoulder, say.
Don't talk to me. I'm dancing.

What I Left

I left: floorboards that squeak, piano with dust
I left: a chair with a blue shirt hung over the back

I left: the TV on in the dark
cop show and all the commercials

I kept: a cardboard box of squash, some pumpkins
I kept: the broken sidewalk

I left: a woman on a highway with a sign:
stop on one side, *slow* on the other

I kept: lazy, clean the cupboards, don't let him down
I kept: sorry I haven't written, I owe you a letter

I kept: can't carry a tune in a basket
suit yourself
tomorrow or the next day
I kept: not worth his salt, not worth his time

I left: leave me alone, too much alone, let it alone, let it go
I kept: watchdog, don't get out of the car
I left: plum brush windfall longhorn angus charolais
I left: original sin confess your sin forgive yourself
he didn't mean anything by it

I kept: Saturday night dance,
don't get the big head, stay in your own pay grade
don't kill bull snakes
don't tell your mother she lies

don't count on it
don't breathe a word

don't kid yourself

I never left

I never kept

anything.

To the Egyptian Scribe

In front of your statue in the museum,
a man in a tee shirt and ball cap
kisses a woman who has

curly hair
in a rubber band
at the nape. She kisses back

and then reads aloud
a sign
which declares a scribe

was an artist,
and pieces of his work
were always placed in his tomb.

Scribe, who died
having loved whatever you loved,
what did you long for?

When she kisses,
her lips curve, compress, flatten,
let go.

When she kisses,
her lips, not wet, not quite dry,
make their sound.

To a Woman in a Room in New York

Room in New York
Edward Hopper, 1882-1967

I've been where you seem to be: the night, the city, the man.
Each of us wears her own

brand of red dress, has one chance,
though chances might seem endless as four walls.

How do you suggest we talk to one another? Piano to
lamp.

The quiet is fine, and the light
on the table and his collar and sleeve. He's fine,

reading his paper.
Your one life

one note you like the sound of.

One note
one note,

you listen for it to change.
There was nothing for me but to

step to that tall brown door
and go.

What I Wanted

What I wanted to say
existed surely in my body somewhere,
in thorax or solar plexus,
or perhaps in the larynx
like wine at the top of the bottle.
What I wanted to say
was that I did what I did
for the best most honorable reason.

No. What I wanted
was to pull my naked body up onto the raft
with minimal loss of skin. What I wanted
was to save myself in your eyes,

to erase, to delete completely
the change I could see in your face—
upper lip accusatory,
each iris frozen.
What I wanted was to run time backward
as I have seen you do with a movie:
the perpetrator undoes the deed, gesture by gesture
in the shadows on the screen, hides the weapon
once more in the folds of her dress.
Her foot in the red boot takes a step back. Another.
Retreat. Retreat. She waits again in the draperies.
What I wanted: a second chance. No. I wanted
a first chance, a beginning, a sky.

I Will Say Sky

I will say *sky*
and hold it,
a huge blue bowl over us in the desert.

I will say *cactus*
and have night fall,

a single headlight star
between the arms of a saguaro.

I will say *dry* and then *not dry,*
the Guadalupe Wash filling with blue water,

emptying again to show white sand
and hundreds and thousands of blue blossoms
like a narrow river through the dry places,

fragrance from those flowers so very light
as to be imaginary

and you, real

and I, real

in a room with six windows,
old soft couch, couch with faded floral print
we sit upon and sink our bodies into
and relax on together,
our cotton shirt lives opening,
our gold foil-wrapped chocolate lives,

opening,
opening.

II

The Bird She Says She Saw

Then the gold was gone from the world
Mark Doty

A child may see a grackle in the sun,
its feathers flickering purple and green.

She may describe this to her father.
Let us say her father loves the truth

and instructs the child
that lying will get her nowhere,

the bird she says she saw
much too crazy for this part of the world.

Meanwhile the grackle continues
across the grass,

reaching each foot forward,
head bobbing,

sun
on its slick black feathers.

Its slick black feathers
a prism

splitting light
into purple and green:

any ordinary thing moving in the world,
striking sparks for the untrained eye.

Nights Were Too Short to Measure

Nights were too short to measure
and you woke in the bed yawning,
arms stretching like thin strong animals—
legs, spine, the big sigh. That was sleep:

narrow strip between one day and the next.
Did you ride the dented bicycle
through the town and out into the country,
cattle on both sides of the road?

Skies you ignored or lay down to look at.
Taste of bromegrass, teeth
crushing the knob of juice in the stem,
the soft yielding inner layer. Sleeping

one kind of sleep when your eyes were open
and another kind at night, the window ajar,

breeze lying over you like a gauze,
pulling back like a curtain.
Hair sweaty at the nape,
arms flung over your head, befitting your fall.

On the Road

My father knew of a store on the highway
where they sold good bologna
so we stopped there—what is better
than a working man on vacation?

It was better than it should be, all of it:
the gray road,
pale hot land rolling by the windows,
two buckskin horses at a fence,

the shine of my young mother's hand
as she cut the bologna with a jack-knife,
the tips of her fingers placing a circle of meat
on the cracker, placing a crumble of cheese,

a woman laughing,
a man in love, driving,
his mouth open to receive
the wafer from her hand.

Argument

My father said Why don't you want to talk about it?
and the straight line of her lips said
she had said all she was going to say;

her flat back in her green sweater said
that was all he was going to hear from her.
He said he couldn't win.

I kept thinking somebody could win
but I couldn't find the starting line in that house.
All week I couldn't find the flags

or the silver trophy or the posted rules of the game.
I found my bedroom and I found books
and a map with the names of rivers

on the crooked blue lines flowing east.
Child, go out the front door.
Find the wind; let it blow your hair across your face

because all night the wind
has been talking, promising *never again*
promising *always always*

and sometimes with little pieces of sleet
touching and touching
the smooth cool cheek of the window.

Template

I saw my father sag down on the stairs,
fold like a couple of sticks
and weep, a few tears

down his face near his nose,
his eyes shut,
his arms at his sides,

and my mother stood
a few feet away
making pie crust in a bowl,

her fingers
pinching flour and Crisco
and the dash of salt.

Her chin
the chin of her one-legged grandfather,
his crutch down and forward

and down again,
crossing the yard to the barn
where he couldn't pitch hay

but could manage,
with cursing and grit,
to milk a Holstein.

My mother can mutter
with her lips practically closed.
My father can cry on the stairs

and none of my words
can lift him
or make my mother's hands

stop shaping and rolling
and turning the flat white circle of pie crust,
dragging it limp through flour.

Education

From her white knuckles I learned
that fear is a thing to hold on to,

as if it had value,
as if it were a calf at the end of a rope.

From her stories I learned
that a plain vanilla life

must be frosted thick with icing,
sliced,

laid on your best plate
and sprayed with fake whipped cream.

From her silences I learned
that small injuries are rubies

to be polished and set into a crown.
Once you learn this, you know it for a long time.

From him
late

stepping over the threshold of the back door
in his work boots,

I learned that tools are faithful,
that work is good.

Work is a totem pole you carve and carve
a lifetime

into a tall column with staring eyes
and fierce faces,

larger and more colorful
than your own.

Retina

My life
moves on the retina
upside down,

this night in spring,
Arcturus a pinpoint
on the curve of a small black curtain.

If I were anywhere
instead of here on the driveway,
running once more away from home—

if I were at the river,
cranes would land
in the small theater of the retina,

flap in the near-dark,
and find a place to settle.
But here is the image of my mother,

inverted, diminished,
windows of her house behind her,
her shoulders round,

arms hanging,
mouth awry,
cheeks wet.

What will I make of this,
of anything?
The fine black lines

of the feet of the cranes
dance upside down
in the globe of the eye.

She recedes, student of broken things.
For me: the windshield and the dash,
my oncoming implacable road.

Fearing Water

Mother, you fear
a day of swimming,

fear the river,
its brown blank face.

I, too.

Is it channels
we dread?

Marriage,
love.

That which draws us in or down,
that which has no hesitation.

For our brief time
we swim side by side

as if creatures with fins.
We keep our round eyes open.
Fear is the watery thing in which we live.

Her Kid Brother Ran Beside the Car

After phoning her father
she caught a ride from the depot.
Her kid brother waited at the bridge
and then ran, grinning, beside the car
all the way to the house.
He was taller and bonier than the day she left,
bib overalls hanging on his shirtless shoulders,
thick dark hair shaking with his running.

He clammed up and backed off when she
got out. She held her squirming baby
and stood at the driver's window to thank
the neighbor who had given her a ride,
a long thanks protocol called for.
Neither father nor mother came to the door,
one reading the county paper
and one peeling an extra potato, and it was
her kid brother who reached for the suitcase
and ran ahead over the cedar needles
to open the heavy door.

We Visit the Homestead

She shows me
the location under the trees

where her father, years ago,
fell dead

beside the buzz saw,
the broken blade in his throat.

Spot of grass
where he lay

when she ran from the house to the grove
and saw him.

Will you stay with the body, someone asked her,
and she did.

Knelt beside the body,
laid her apron over his face.

The body dressed as it was in chore clothes, layers
of shirts, heavy coat.

No gloves, the better to guide the wood
to the blade.

The body
needing work, needing cattle,

a horse to ride, a barn to build,
as if work were food and drink:

lift this, carry this,
never put it down.

Stay.
The body, marvelous when bending,

beautiful carrying, kneeling, hammering,
exquisite the movement, the dance.

Her hands on my shoulders, she turns me to face her.
There are wrinkles accordion on her upper lip.

You can always, she tells me—
her lips pursing and flexing—her teeth small, gray—

You can always do what you have to do.

Finally I Ask

Finally I ask if I can carry
what she carries, part of it,
and she gives over a brown paper bag.

She leans against the side of the house
and looks at me, steady.
Her eyes are what I will remember.

The incredible weight of the burden.
Nobody needs this, I say. *Let's leave it here;*

we'll never miss it,
this lead and feathers combo,

this cockamamie shield
we hold heart-high.

Her eyes do not change
from watchful. Mine,
from her angle, must be the same.

Stand-In

My mother, on her back, struck at the nurses
during the ambulance ride. *Combative*

was the word they checked on their form.
She tried to black their eyes.

She didn't use her famous silent treatment,
so successful so many times;

she used her fists, those old crumpled leaves,
and she aimed at what was above her.

She slapped the best schools,
the up market, the down market,

the classmate
who wore the red sash on the white dress.

She scratched at the woman who could waltz,
the one who had the pretty laugh.

Just this once the handsome face of money
hung almost within reach

of her work-red short-nail bad-luck hands.
Combative, the nurse tells me, and I say *I'm sorry,*

but a part of me I usually ignore
speaks up;

a part of me I often discount
says, *No you're not.*

Artifact

At the museum,
I walk among displays:
beaded moccasins and arrowheads.

I think about women
dropping meat
into boiling water,

feeding children
corn or hope or milk,
a mother opening her garment

so a baby can suck his fill,
his head between the warmth of her body
and the skin of the deerskin dress.

In a hospital room,
standing at the sink
on my substantial legs,

I wash my mother's dentures,
scrubbing
uppers and lowers,

artificial pink
artificial white
under running water.

My dripping fingers
place her teeth
into a curved plastic dish,

and, I carry it,
an offering,
toward her bed.

She Was Perhaps Dead

She was perhaps dead
and the pacemaker kept her heart pumping.
Her eyes stared like nothing I'd seen
and her jaw clamped; she was biting her lip.
The nurses, knowing where to press,
made her let go somehow.
She never blinked. She stared
like an actress in a silent movie.
The hospice staff knew
how to turn the pacemaker off,
my sisters holding a magnet
over the device under the skin
of her thin chest.
I stood away and cried.
There is much I can do
but I couldn't do that,
though I touched her skin
before and after it was cold,
laid my warm palms
on her hands.
You worked hard, Mom, I said,
and I said *Thank you.*
I held my sisters while they cried.
One, then the other
in my arms—
I held those who had held her.

I Didn't Know I Loved

I didn't know I loved her big hands
slicing iceberg lettuce
with a thick-bladed knife,

loved her thumb hooked over the lip
of the shallow melmac bowl
she carried to the table.

Low-class no-class entrees
like her swiss steak,
her bean soup in a kettle.

She posed in shorts and a halter top,
goosebumps
on her untanned legs.

My father loved her,
carried the photograph away to war,
brought it back.

I didn't know I loved open country,
prairie grass,
miles and miles of sky.

The coyote's unstudied lope across the field.
The badger's un-pretty teeth,
its front door a hole in the gully.

My mother made cottage cheese.
Why did I never tell you this before?

She left the bowl of milk overnight on the counter,
added rennet.
I sprinkled sugar on the clots and ate it.

I didn't know I loved the head of the nail,
the blow of the hammer,
blueprint become the shell of the house.

The foot into the same shoe each morning
six days a week,
leather taking the contour of arch.

I didn't know I loved
the way a red-tailed hawk
will sit in a tree, waiting

to swoop down and to crush
any live warm thing that will nourish.

The Women of My Family

kill snakes with a hoe,
leave the head, opening and closing,
leave the body whipping itself into coils in the row of beets.
These women make their choices and stay,
their husbands wearing overalls and brown lace-up boots
smelling of pig barn. *Don't wear those filthy clothes in my house*
my women say
and the offender must go to the basement to take off the stench
and come up the stairs in his underwear, carrying his boots to the porch.

My women scrape cake batter into a pan,
tap it a couple of times on the counter,
and slide it into a hot oven. My women make pickles:
heat brine, pour it into jars,
screw the lids on. Any woman of mine
can twist the lid tight enough to last the winter.
One of them gives me bread from the oven, the slice
toppling slowly into her hand while she cuts the loaf.
She stores salt in a heavy glass dish in the cupboard
so she can reach in and get a pinch to
sprinkle over eggs in a skillet.

Every Monday she cleans the clothesline,
running a rag over it,
the hand with the rag raised above her head,
her feet treading the ground. And that is how
I will remember her, one fist skyward, walking.
Now she shakes out a shirt and hangs it. It fills like a sail
and she lays her hand lightly on its cotton back
before she goes on.

Within

When I was lodged within my mother
I floated as she walked to work,
bobbing at anchor, insulated from any bump in the road,
and later wedged in tightly, not able to stretch,
well-fed, warm in an upside-down world.
You, too,
floated in your water world,
finishing at last with that space, or lack of it,
squeezed through an aperture,
not to be upside down much again
except a time or two in the grass,
rolling head over heels—small remnant.
By our own biped laws walking
as soon as we are able, the liquid world
shut to us except as swimmers, visitors
to pools or to oceans, and perhaps
with luck and planning to a small flotation chamber,
a rented darkness,
water in which large quantities of salts
have been dissolved, a door to close
for an hour, body floating face-up,
water the temperature of the skin,
ears below water listening only to water,
hearing the breath in,
the breath out.
No wonder we want this dark chamber—
and fear it—water holding the body,
our own pulse an approximation
of the drum of the mother's heart, first music,
the beat she always had for us, walking to work,
walking home again, hungry or tired in the world

we eventually come into, when the time comes.
The attendant knocks on the door. The hour's up.
And the body rises,
opens with its own two hands the door,
and there is light now. The body emerges and begins:
shower, dress, and return—because it's time—
to the world of work.

Labor

My mother picked up a piece of clotted blood,
wiped it from the floor with a Kleenex,
a motion of stooping down and scooping up.
She followed me down the hall
of the small-town hospital

and she probably knew the names of the people
in the chairs in the waiting area, but I didn't.
I knew only the pains of labor
and that I had been waiting hours and hours
for all this to be over,

no husband holding my hand,
and I walked the hall
because the nurse thought walking might help.
I held my back and held my front,
that hobbling holding groaning posture of motherhood

and motherhood also following it,
mopping up its spill,
its red stain
while the doctor
goes home for Sunday dinner. Motherhood is

pain in regular increments:
something to be stayed with,
to be trailed in its wobbly circles,
its keening cry followed,

until it can lie carefully and heavily down and deliver.

Textile

Where are those scraps
which warmed us?
Women's work

quilts are, and do not last.
Steel persists,
and silver.

Cotton goes the way of rivers,
snowbanks,
footprints,

sweethearts, all of it
mere embroidery.
Cotton is mortal,

takes meaning
from the threads
around it,

travels over and under,
breaks open,

burns,
exhales,

gives its ash to air.

III

Last Time We Had Blood All Over

Last time we had blood all over the carpet
so this time my daughter and I

decide the kitchen floor
will be better for this. When I call,

the dog comes out from hiding
under the bed. I love the dog

a hundred-fold that moment.
What could be holier than a black dog

lowering her head
for the one who wants to cut her nails?

My daughter, afraid she will slip with the nippers
and cut into the quick as she did last time,

is anxious. I say things to calm her
and to calm myself, hold the dog in my arms,

belly up, a giant clam shell,
paws flopped over. A divine thing,

not struggling at all.
The wet blue cloth I drape over her eyes

shows the shape of her head
and I concentrate on that

and listen for the snap of the tool,
for the tick of each black nail
when it hits the tiles.

For My Body

Belly, thank you, holding whatever grief I feed on.
What to do with the corn chips, the almonds, the late-night bread?

Arms: hanging on until you crumble.
Neck: stiff, afraid of plunder.

Spine and ribs, all my bones,
lusty, involved.

All pouches, blossoms, chutes, sinews, cul-de-sacs, seedpods
waiting for harvest, thank you.

The son you bore
drove up and parked in front of the house at Christmas.

How giddy, how foolish the body
leaving the kitchen, the food roasting or boiling or waiting,

metatarsals shoeless
down the sidewalk to greet him,

iris and pupil and retina
working as if to remember this:

his body in his gray parka, getting out of the car,
keys in his hand,

his arms reaching to hold
as your arms reach to hold.

Body: storehouse of the infinite,
giddy, foolish, forgiven.

Pinning His Hand

My son e-mails, hunting and pecking,
that he has injured his hand.
I did it playing kickball he says
but I am telling my friends
I was pulling children from a burning building.
A joke from this intense and serious man—
was he ever tiny enough to lodge inside me—
do I know him at all?
I hit *reply*, telling him to take care of his body
as if it were his beloved child.
Which it is,
which he is,
mine,
that child in the kitchen,
for whom I made chocolate chip cookies.
He's only three years old
and wants to see the cookie dough
so I lift him to the counter,
seat him beside the mixer.
I place him next to danger
so he can see the slippery eggs
easing into butter and sugar,
he who builds his own deck
on the north side of his house
he who goes down to the river
on Fridays after work
and bikes with his dog
on the trail for hours
his young mother so young, so much
the fool,
so much the loner.

I would take better care of you
I would do better
you who have moved away
and take care of yourself.
Take care of yourself I tell the sky
over the trees in his general direction
the morning the surgery is slated,
the doctor scrubbed and informed,
taking I think my sleeping son's hand
into his own
some unknown surgeon

standing in for the mother
and in some expert way
with deliberate patient skill
pinning the broken places.

Here's to My Legs

Here's to my knees, especially the left one
and the small grating sound it makes
when I lie on the beach and bicycle it above me,
slow in the sun.

A blessing of sorts on my ankles, which are thick
(I refuse to curse them anymore)
and do not forget the fat sleek toes,
nails painted red, those shameless dancing girls.

Here's to shins
playing straight man to the calves.
Thighs browning, shiny with oil.
Let the bottom of each foot
have its time on hot sand.

Let the feet take all the body to the water,
let the legs look around below sea level, let them
kick, cavort, mislead;
let the ocean have them for its one split tongue.

How I Would Paint

after Lisel Mueller

AGE

A workhorse with wide haunches,
her brown teeth biting the bit.
She is locked behind a door in the barn.

MARRIAGE

I'd paint yellow flowers but I'd paint over them
a river with gray boulders and froth.
I'd paint over that:
cranes in a field,

some with spots of red on their crowns,

some dancing, leaping up to show off,

one bringing a stone to lay in front of another.

DEATH

A lake, smooth, a green bank,
and I'd paint eyes, wide open
in the mirror of the water.

To the Writers

I wanted to bring myself perfectly calm
to sit by the gray river.
I wanted to bring you what I had accomplished,
what I had worked over, polished, seen clearly, saved.

I wanted to bring you a wise saying,
a pretty string of words like birdsong
to make you love me for a moment.
I wanted to carve from a bar of white soap.
I wanted to fashion a fish so ideal you would say *Ahhh*.
Its scales I wanted to shape so you would adore me,
so you would think *This fish can swim*.

I wanted to bring you my old faded face for kissing.
I wanted to come clear-eyed but last night I couldn't rest;
the curtains in my room I memorized at midnight and 2 a.m. and 3 a.m.

That thing I promised I would do without fail for you
I have failed to do.
One of the words you gave me I have placed under a flat stone in the garden.

Butterflies came last week to a cottonwood near my house
as you might have known they would.
As you might have known they would, they clung with their delicate feet
to the surfaces they found.
They were new leaves of the tree. They held on as if it were their plan.
Not one of them could see the whole.
They were each
one leaf
and could not see the tree.

To the writers: I wanted to be important.
I wanted to be grand, substantial, nourishing, wise.
I am too close to see what we have made
and are now making.

I Want to Be a Man

I want my voice deep out of my chest,
water welling up in a spring. Hard water, rock
dissolved in it. A good-looking man, why not?
I want excellent teeth. Tough skin, like leather.
Why not, why the hell not?
I want a beard. I want shirts. I want biceps.
I want to play basketball as if it mattered,
pound down the court, life or death.
My hair in a pony tail
over my collar, or maybe no hair at all.
I want to take my guitar out of the case,
thread my arm and neck through the strap,

sing a baby-baby song. I want to cook,
want to chop onions with a big knife, chop fast,
as the onion and the knife and the board
seem to need. I want to cook four-alarm chili, I want to
eat it. I want to eat jalapeño. I want to sweat.
On my legs I want hair—I mean *hair*, I mean
bristles. Whatever I carry—the plates, the ladder, the log—
will be light as peanuts.

I don't want to be a man.
Oh, I want the shirt and the sweat and the chilies,
the chest hair and baby-baby. I want that, as I want all.
I want to weep, man and woman, and to be done weeping,
filled and empty at the same time.
Man and woman and animal and vegetable and mineral,
I want to write my songs. I want to break open,
a papaya full of black seeds. I want to pour out
red as wine into raised cups.

You Can't Say I

Resist much.
Walt Whitman

Imagine the authorities telling us we can't say *I.*
Imagine the fines I'll have to pay:
500 for *I will,* 500 for *I want,* 500 for
Do I?

And then the next decree
comes down: no *my,* no *mine.*
You, *my* friend, friend of *mine,*
may have a stash of *I* and *me*
jingling around like quarters

but authority can clip a hole in the pocket of your blue jeans
with sharp silver scissors. You still have a *Could I* and a *Should I*
hidden in one pair of shoes,
under the arch supports.
Walk around on that.

There have always been people telling us you can't say *I.*
What do they say, *I* wonder, to their mirrors in the morning
or when they sit in their meetings?

There have always been people like us, common as grass,
who stand with the best posture they can muster
and sometimes hold hands or link arms
and walk down the road
hearing a beat in the body,
one foot saying *I,* the other saying *we.*

Mammogram

My name is Maggie, she says, *and I'll be*
doing your mammogram today.
Maggie all day in a windowless room
saying dozens of times: *I'm just*
going to have you step up here—now if you'll
turn a little to your right, put your arm here.

She lifts my left breast, the one with vague densities
my doctor wants a closer look at. She lays it
on a cold steel shelf.
Her foot presses a switch; a piece of Plexiglas,
a colorless flat hand,

whines down, thins my breast,
flattens it under plastic into a fat living capital A,
the nipple stretched like a maroon stocking cap
at the top of big A.
Maggie's foot taps, the A spreads,
big A, bigger A, humongous A.
How's that? she asks.
Don't breathe, she says

and steps behind her shield, pushes buttons.
You can breathe now, she says,
but I have been, a little, all along, for luck.
She is going to show these to the radiologist
and would I wait right here?
In my tissue paper gown, I wait.
I half take off the gown and do my own exam:
you look good to me; you look fat and sleek
and happy as a baby,

you with three black dots
where Maggie marked with her felt-tip.
Hey you, I say, *you're good. You're both OK.*

Sure enough Maggie comes back and she says
Everything's fine. And though
I think she means the x-rays are readable, not fuzzy,
I'll take it.
Yes, Maggie, I'm fine. Both right and left,
I'm fine past the lady at Information.

I'm fine out the revolving door.
Fine on South 27th,
and fine at Commercial Federal where the cashier—
who under her blue jacket is probably a 38 or 40D—
asks me how I am today.

And re-inflated, having found in a pocket early this morning
an old check I forgot to cash,
and having cashed it,
and having the day off,
and having the left and right in all their densities
against my favorite washed-out purple shirt,

and having no stainless steel Plexiglas call-backs
for at least six months,
I tell the cashier: I'm fine,
I'm truly fine.

Loony As a Squirrel, I'm Trespassing on My Neighbor's Lawn

God called unto him out of the midst of the bush . . .
Exodus 3:4

I trespass across my neighbor's grass
until I reach my neighbor's late-autumn fire-red burning bush

until I'm next to it, cheek by jowl,
and it is burning mightily, O each red leaf is burning
curled in flame
and not consumed

and I am
(might as well confess what the Almighty,
if the Almighty is in the neighborhood, can see already)

actually

in it

in the very burning bush.

I want—if it's possible—to see the divine in the burning bush.

No—check that—I want to see what the divine can see
from the self-same burning bush.

I see what every passerby sees: you driving the street on your errand, you
late for work, you hollering at your kid
and I see pin oaks

rising from the ground like a dozen columns of a temple

I see—check that—I *feel*

a light rain descending

I hear two dogs harrumphing

I hear tuning-up starlings and boss-man jays

I see my neighbor's last rose, pink around the gills

and his mums: round mound of brownish gold

the coiffure of his hostas, blond with green roots

the finny locust finery against the wet black branches

the gingko ripe, just about to dump a load of paydirt
into the lap of the lawn

I see leaves like lizard hands this way and that
on the long sloping sidewalk

I see a handful of leaves at the end of one of the arms of the nearest
        nearly red oak
moving in wind as if to spirit—that is: (1) to carry off mysteriously or
        (2) to impart courage, animation, or determination to—

moving as if to *spirit* this lovely living world.

I see I'll have to move my headquarters.
There being untold unplumbed value in goofiness,
I'm going to have to check this out:
perhaps the divine is in the moving on.

Resurrection

After the spring snowstorm
I go out to save trees, shaking them
as if they were sleepers,
hanging on when they lift,
standing in waterfalls of snow,
my hair awash with it,
earrings cold on my neck.

I crack off a dead limb from the redbud
and use it, a scepter, on the pines,
my face up to snow coming down,
mouth open to eat,
glasses covered, snow behind the lenses,
wet snatches burning my cheeks
where I brushed against the needles.

I turn back toward the house: an old man stumbling,
my jacket whitened,
my arms straight,
hands numb.
A grin on my blind face,
I walk the drifts, chanting:

Rise.

Rise.

You and I, the Morning

Mornings are
faithful dogs who settle on the rug with a sigh.

In the next room you eat your bowl of grapenuts,
you have your headlines.

In this room, the dark.
The windows and, at a distance,

the full moon of a streetlight
cut to pieces by trunks and branches.

Yesterday I heard an owl above the roof.
I called to you, made you come

to hear it:
over our heads six wavering notes.

Today I could—
but don't—

call you to witness
one star in a black tree.

Alone—like me—
one glittering far-flung silent bird.

In Praise of Pursed Lips

Praise those who kiss
with the lips pursed,
those who have not learned kissing

from celebrities
nibbling the upper or lower lip.
Those who first kiss dry

and then melt, the purse strings loosened,
those who kiss for the kiss of it,
not on a payroll of any kind,

unless bacon and eggs is a payroll
and a kitchen is a movie set;
praise of the perfunctory,

that which gets one started, and
praise the flannel shirt over the belly,
praise the belly.

This is in praise
of breasts
and of rib bones

and of thigh against thigh,
straight as young tree trunks,
thighs part of the kiss

as the back is part of the kiss,
and the vigor of arms. This is in praise
of the faint aroma of the skin of the face;

this is for faint, and for inexhaustible;
this is in praise of the pursed kiss
and the long one that follows and opens and stays.

The Women in the Pool

I have but one voice. I have but one.
My songs might reach farther than I can,
but I am just one.
                    Pam Herbert Barger

We keep our heads above water Fridays at 5:00
in the long blue pool at the Y.
We are here to exercise, to find our range of motion.

We do the scissors, do the crab, talk our talk.
We say: *Pammo, sing something.*
And she will, if she feels like it:

I have but one voice. I have but one.
My songs might reach farther than I can,
but I am just one.

Stretch, crab, scissors,
the knees-together thing we call the Jerry Lewis.
We can't see our bellies, our cellulite. We don't care at all.

What is best is when we fall quiet,
water's small clean hands
clapping our shoulders.

Things That Do Not Matter

The Monarch emerges wet from its shell
and hangs by delicate feet. A drop

of wing-dye falls. Excess,
always excess. Scattered on the continent

are dried pools of womb-water
from this or that body,

the last of the yolk, the extra dram
from the birth.

These do not matter
in the way moonrise

above the ocean
at this moment

makes no difference.
The hand of the sea

at this moment
washes the rocks,

and at this moment,
recedes.

How Shall the Heart?

*How shall the heart be reconciled
to its feast of losses?*
Stanley Kunitz

I walked the floors of universities,
wrinkles deepening over my knucklebones,

one long hair after another falling to lie
on the shoulders of my shirts. When I look behind

at the milestone parties, white wine catching light,
late-night conversation face to face,

crackers and cheese on a paper plate,
reason and rebuttal over which I hovered,

when I see how we ate and drank words, see us
small and earnest at the wrong end of a spyglass,

I long for more of that music.
Talk to me; bring me ideas:
curled pink shrimp and a dish of red sauce.

One Finger Wave

I say silly things like *Hi, Honey* to Lake Superior
when I round a curve on U.S. 61 and there she is.

Hi, Honey to millions of cubic feet of water and bedrock.
I greet celestial bodies like old friends: *How you doin'*

to the full moon. *Good to see you again.*
A momentary camaraderie, an interstice,

a greeting between wayfarers

like the one-finger wave between ranchers
on the roads through the sandhills of Nebraska.

My car, going north,
meets a cattle truck loaded with Angus, going south.

At the proper moment,
the proper distance,

my hands still on the wheel,
I raise my index finger

and the stranger does the same
as if to say:

In our most solitary orbits
we are sometimes not alone.

Listen, My Bearded One

Listen, my broad shoulder, my no-answer answer,
my no mule stubborn as, my forgive me again again,

let's stay with this cross-country we've begun,
this night train, this knick knack paddy whack.

I hardly know my own reflection in the window.
I hardly know the name of the next station.
Do you?

After (or because of) the silent treatment
and the same old same old,

but ahead of No Brain Left At All,
let's fall together in our sleeper car.

There is a way called Muddling Through.
Let's do it our way, me and you.

Fruit to Last

Apples she slices
into thin half-moons

and arranges with her knobby fingers
on a flat pan

which she slides into the oven.
They dry to a brown leather. She tries

to convince me:
they will be tasty this winter.

Pears she instructs me to wrap in newspaper,
each pear enclosed,

a swirl of newsprint, a drape, a shroud;
shapes layered into a basket.

Store them, she says,
in the cellar

and I do,
but not all.

This one,
cool round weight in the palm,

this one I redeem,
I bring into the afterlife,

its blossom on the twig
riding the north wind,

the rain it drank,
the morning light it lived in.

Incisors through the yellow skin,
white meat, dripping, into my mouth,

on my lips and chin,
the juices.

We Leave the ATM Before Dawn

When we leave the ATM before dawn,
clutching new twenties,
when we drive toward the sandhills country,

when the road becomes a two-lane,
when we are upbeat for no good reason
except maybe two travel mugs
of very hot coffee and cream and cocoa
like you make it,

when the tip into daylight
is about to happen,

when grasslands begin to show
in the windows,

then I like to imagine our lives in front of us
ticking under the belly of the car
as we eat up the road. Look,
there's more,
more.
Our life together moving like that, you
believing in me, I believing in you.
Fragile we're not. Speed is where it's at.

We face what's coming:
grasslands parting like a sea
on either side of the asphalt.
We roar past; we leave little farmhouses
bobbing in our wake, trees swirling.
You and me, Babe,
you and me, immortals on a road trip.

About the Poet

Marjorie Saiser was named Distinguished Artist in Poetry by the Nebraska Arts Council in 2009. Her books are *Bones of a Very Fine Hand* (1999) and *Lost In Seward County* (2001), both from The Backwaters Press, and also a chapbook, *Moving On,* from Lone Willow Press (2002). Her awards include the Nebraska Literary Heritage Award, the Nebraska Book Award, the Leo Love Award, The Vreelands Award, and an award from the Academy of American Poets. Saiser's poems have been published in *Prairie Schooner, Georgia Review, Crab Orchard Review, Cream City Review, Field,* and *Smartish Pace.* She is co-editor of *Times of Sorrow/Times of Grace,* an anthology of writing by women of the Great Plains, and co-editor of *Road Trip,* a book featuring interviews of a dozen Nebraska writers. Her web site is *poetmarge.com.* She and her husband, Don, live in Lincoln, Nebraska.

CPSIA information can be obtained at www.ICGtesting.com
Printed in the USA
240392LV00003B/35/P

9 781935 218173